After
Thunder
poetry from the edge of
fatherhood and ALS

Bob Seltzer

AF471778

*After Thunder* by Bob Seltzer



Printed in the United States of America

Cover Art: "BrainSky" by Megan Laurel

First Edition

ISBN: 978-1-300-17257-4

CONTENTS


| | |
|---|---|
| Insane Asylum | 7 |
| Land Mines | 9 |
| Runt | 10 |
| Seesaw | 11 |
| After Thunder | 13 |
| Vaccination | 14 |
| Rocking Horse | 15 |
| Papa's Ant | 17 |
| My Amazing Boy | 18 |
| Nature-Nurture | 19 |
| Academia | 20 |
| Emission | 21 |
| Normandy | 22 |
| Moving On | 23 |
| Brainfart | 25 |
| Generation Gap | 26 |
| To the Moon, and Back | 27 |
| Sea World | 28 |
| Squeak Toy | 29 |
| Smallville Parade | 30 |
| Snakes | 31 |
| Red Cross | 32 |
| Re-Orientation | 33 |
| Windmills | 35 |
| Awareness | 36 |
| Twenty-Five Words (or Fewer) | 37 |
| Mr. Snuggles | 38 |
| Morpheus | 39 |

Doctor 40
My First Time 42
Any Given Sunday 43
Venus Transit 44
Tuskegee 45
Others 46
Hook(s) 47
Head Games 48
Rubber Duckie 49
Helium Day 50

Thanks go out to Kate
(for diligently and politely showing me how I can't write),
Deirdre (My Love), Liam and Maeve (My Inspiration),
Frank (for making poetry real), KMA (for making this book real)
and, finally, Writing Circle
("Our Drinking Circle with a Writing Problem").

*Nunc est Bibendum*

## Insane Asylum (or Aristotle as Thorazine)

We should thank The Philosopher
for reminders of context—i.e.,
only some situations invoke
concern. Anxiety with gun barrel,
good; with uncapped toothpaste,
bad.

Submitted: an individual sits,
eyes-wide, looking nowhere, one-hand
shaking a doll, screaming at nothing,
then laughing.

(Psychotic)

Submitted: another (slightly older),
eyes-half-open, unintentional muse,
looking at nothing, saying to no one
in particular:
*We have to fill out the paperwork.*

(Schizophrenic)

Endless incantations; short, sharp,
biting comments on character
and possession that instantly dissolve;
extreme bipolar temperaments diffusing
in the presence of shiny distractions;
imaginary friends with real desires;
declarations of memory that flicker
between detailed and absent—
and so on.

Yes, we should all remember to thank
The Philosopher for reminders
of the context
of childhood.

## Land Mines

No one could blame the house;
it had seen too much life.
Built long ago, absorbing
Wars and Depression,
its only job was to
Endure and Perform.

Time, however, is problematic:
the wearing of joints,
the sounds of decay,
the worn wrinkles,
the creaking laugh-lines—
the stairs from hell,
the floors from purgatory.

A sleeping toddler is antithetical,
reactive, dispositional, and new—
opposed to a tenured house,
to the absence of silence
from a house glad
to have persevered.

Happy houses require subtle
avoidance of displaced areas
of jovial detonation—
in avoiding nocturnal laughter,
foolish contortion-walks are
always more appealing than
insomnious neonate nights.

## Runt

The rumbling of The Pack
shook the back deck in summertime;
infinite pairs of approaching sneakers
(I heard them before I saw them),
screams, growls, and yells—the
socially oblivious tourbillion
turning the corner, the boom
dissipating—slowly.

Count to four…

Two sneakers, inchoate and infinitesimal—
(I heard them before I saw them)—
*pit-pat-pit-pat*,
faint and slow by comparison,
attached to a tiny body,
arms extended, at sides, head down,
eyes locked-on-feet, trying to run
(but not quite there), oblivious,
turning the corner with intense
purpose, barely keeping balance.

The dedicated, faithful
tail—determined to be
where the kite
once was, yet always
trailing behind

(for now).

## Seesaw (an exercise in writing a children's book)

It is Christmas time.
My daughter is adorable.

It is awkward. It is difficult.
I am reading. It is horrible.
I am reading something horrible.

A couple where one
is about to die.
About the final
moments in the hospital.
Waiting for the end
and then the post-end.
Very detailed. Very disturbing.
I am there.

I love my wife very much.
I do not want her to die.
It is bothering me.
I also love my daughter.
She is adorable.

It is awkward.

She runs back and forth,
in and out of the room,
singing "Jingle Bells"—
the part where we all
say, *Hey!*
The part that everyone likes.

I see the story, see my wife dying,
then dead.
I see my daughter,
young, fresh, full of life.
Running back and forth,
back and forth.
Smiling wildly, loving the moment.

I do not want her to think something is wrong.
I know she'll see me and wonder.
I do not want that.
I want her to feel alive.
I do not want her to feel the death
I am feeling.

I switch on and off, on and off,
pretending to laugh.

It is awkward.

## After Thunder

The first time I ever saw
my daughter's face after thunder,
I wanted to tell her it was okay,
the sky wasn't going to fall and
kill her, and she didn't do anything
wrong.

I wanted to tell her she shouldn't
think of it as if she were Eve fleeing
the Garden (expelled with or without
regret) for discovering what would
curse Eve and her children forever.

I wanted her to know she wasn't
about to be punished, the world didn't
judge her, and no one rejected her—
at least not yet.

The sound, I wanted to tell her, was
really more like a hiccup or a sneeze,
instantaneous and annoying, as opposed
to other things more
important and eternal—
like my love for her.

## Vaccination

The infant lies,
relaxed, aware of only
the soft feeling
of hands,
slowly, gently
gripping, coercing.

Air the temperature
of blood as two
scrub-violators
reveal their
medical bayonets.

At stab-impact, the
eyes tell all:
shock, pain, anger—
and for some, betrayal,
disappointment,
sadness.

No one should doubt
the benefits;
the problem
lies rather
in the method
of delivery.

## Rocking Horse (Insane Asylum II)

The grocery store is an awful place;
it's not clear why people go there.
We know that rocking can be soothing,
and that motion calms the sleep-deprived—
but for countless aisles of food in a foodless world,
maybe just being in the presence of an obscene variety
of food paralyzes as it soothes. And distracts.
*The grocery store as rocking horse,*
*as a way to pass the time.* Customers at the
Chinese buffet get their international culinary
knock-offs for one-third the price, and they fail to notice,
or succeed in avoiding, the chopsticks—which is weird
because, like me, they must have accidentally taken
more than two Q-tips® out of the container after a shower.
(But maybe they just fail to notice, or succeed in avoiding,
what they can do.)

Artificial lights, artificial organization (who knew that
batteries and asparagus were so closely related?), and
temporarily artificial, item-defined people, snagged away
from their lives and signatures and now waiting and looking around with
incessant-background-checkout-beeps. *We all need to eat, so it levels*
*the field.* The category "human"—reduced to a beep.

Rocking and infants go hand in hand, too—
although infants and grocery stores clearly don't.
I hear their cries, and I think, *That makes sense here.*
Motion becomes soothing; parents become
crying extinguishers. But when one invokes rocking,
when one instinctively morphs into a rocking horse,

one should be sure—if only for one's sanity—
that one actually has an infant in one's possession.
I see a person rocking in response to the cries, and then
catching himself quickly, smiling to himself,
wondering if anyone saw him. I am about to tell him
*I've been there, I know what it's like to catch myself*
*in some artificial robotic habit*, when I am
artificially and robotically interrupted…

*…beep…*

## Papa's Ant

At Papa's house, one time,
along with summertime variables
of frisbees, flowers, and nice walks,
a child of mine brought
an ant to me—
so proud and happy,
distracted by the discovery
of independent movement,
of something animate in
non-human form—
oblivious, of course,
to that pinch-force,
enough to pop the hind-half,
and leave it in a state
of half-animation.

## My Amazing Boy (age 9)

When he speaks to me,
time stops and it's just the two of
us, protected momentarily from the
assholes of the world, as if what
he's about to say comes from the
purest part of humanity—and when
he's asked a question and looks up
(to think before answering), I know
that, even if he's wrong, the answer
will come from a person smarter than
Einstein, and with better intentions than
Gandhi (even when they were his age).

But the best time he speaks to me is
when he holds me close and talks into
my side or stomach, when my body muffles
and translates his words so that, however
muted, they are clear and majestic, as if
served on a platinum platter.

And when he speaks to me, I never want
to stop listening, because hearing his
thoughts and observations makes me feel,
in that moment, so special,
I know I will remember and
relive this moment
forever.

## NATURE-NURTURE

My son, age nine, sits at
the dinner table, begins to
do something before eating
I used to do, but haven't done
for centuries; something so
foreign—so familiar—I couldn't
help but stare (for verification):
hands clasped together, nose
touching hands, eyes closed. After
a moment, eyes open, a glance in
my direction, a look of guilt— as if
the exposure of this transcendental
attempt to make his spirit soar
would result in being grounded.

I look down at my food, pretending
not to care, though I can't help but
wonder if he's trying it out, like
some new idea overheard from a
playground conversation.

Even in avoiding incriminating
indoctrination, it turns out different
sources emanate other, and
more important, things—
like curiosity.

## Academia

A far away land,
teeming with ideas,
confrontations,
rebirths, reorganizations—
comforting to the few who
exist on conflict,
subtlety, logic, and
aesthetic judgment.

Upon landing, however,
one should be careful
to watch out for debris.

## Emission

*for D*

Our sweat shows power, the capacity
of heat that our bodies need to release,
a lubrication for, and evidence of, our
rapturous frenzy. I watch you and your
body afterward, watch the tiny droplets
slowly roll down your beautiful crevices
and places where my tongue once was—
and delight in our temporary ambiguity,
knowing no distinction between where
my residual liquid ends and yours begins.

## Normandy

The assault begins at dawn,
the bombs fall as rain,
pounding the grassy shores,
causing the *oligochaeta* to
flee for their lives.

Upon success, some fall to
premature aeronautic
vulnerabilities, while others
fall to various bipedal causes.

Afterward, the dissected carnage
covers the ground, recognized—
and then promptly forgotten.

## Moving On

My father once thought
that birds had hollow feet,
and that was the reason why
they could sit on power lines
without being electrocuted.

My mother once thought
that parents should teach
their children to walk away
from bullies,
because teaching
your children
to defend themselves
would inevitably lead them
to think it was okay
to beat up other kids.

My parents both thought
that swimming right after eating
would result in cramps—
cramps so severe they
would result in
drowning.

I don't know if they
still believe these myths
(I have never asked them),
but, at least so far, the word "jinx"
does not have any place
in my children—

and I smile
as I notice this,
while we all dance around
the living room
with open umbrellas.

## Brainfart

A driver at an intersection,
stopped in his vehicle, adrift
in a sea of minivan-details, waiting (for
some reason) for a stop sign to
turn green.

## Generation Gap

An aged father bends, painfully,
not having done so for some time.
Wiping the dust from inside The Cabinet,
he extracts the last bottle, vodka half-full,
and, looking at the label, recalls the fun,
the flirtations, the absences, the catacombs,
and the residues. How the clear and potent
liquid gave him both rapture and headaches,
calming and releasing him through various
proximal passings.

As if his shift was done and his tour of duty
over, he turns to his son and, after a practiced
speech, offers the bottle with pride, trying to
arm his offspring with parental advice
and responsibility through the passing of a torch.

His son's reply reminds him of parental
limitations, failure of omniscience, those
stuttering moments of myopia causing temporary
humility and frustration:

*Dad, that's water.*

## To the Moon and Back

Looking up to the Moon,
to the vastness of space,
pre-emptively launched to
contemplate the emptiness
of speeding through
three hydrogen atoms
per cubic centimeter, the endless
cycle of imploding stars, immense
gravitational fields, time dilation,
black holes consuming
stars and planets, failed
galaxies, the dance of rock—
barely solidifying a starting
point for the myriad
possibilities of phenotypical
variations, the velocity and
trajectory of civilizations, and
the massive competition
for existence and meaning—

followed by instantaneous touchdown
through involuntary auditory reception
of sound waves in a familiar medium:

*Supper, kids, then Wal-Mart.*

## Sea World

*for Shamu*

Deep beneath the surface of
the ebb and flow of smiling waves
(of applause) lies a vapidly arrogant
species, innocuously existing in a
cheesy cesspool of (forced)
Broadway shows maliciously
distracting—(in)directly reaffirming
How Wonderful We Are (through
casting-calls for lower mammals);
the mating calls of marketability—
the only way to find real value
in something? Make it a Movie Star.

## Squeak Toy

Our infant
approaches the object
with fascinated curiosity,
as something that behaves
and speaks a language
yet to be understood, alive and
needing to be investigated, probed,
and analyzed—eventually transformed
into an imaginative companion,
playmate, a being with preferences,
predictably filtered and sanitized.

Our canine
approaches the object
as prey, antagonistic, defiant,
needing to be subdued by
mutilation; the inescapable, inferred
sounds of pain and suffering, of
howling with each escaping draft,
correlated with every jaw-vise-pulse,
exacerbating exponentially its
appetite for blood, culminating in
the thrashing slaughter of
plastic insubordination.

## Smallville Parade

The procession began early,
the dew was almost gone
from the grass; illuminated
trees for blocks, volunteers,
smiles, horse dung, mini-flags,
mini-guns, and Shriner-mini-cars
following the predictable trail
to nowhere.

Nestled between the fire department
and cheerleaders was a beverage
truck, a rolling commercial for
bottled water, employees throwing
the bottles to the
curbside-couch-potatoes
like candy—

a sight bewildering
indeed to those
third-world and parched.

## Snakes

I have never been one against
the color green, or shamrocks,
and I've always been one who
submits to the power of music—
bagpipes or otherwise.

But I find it hard to ignore
that a day such as this, like
so many other days that play
the role of a holiday flyer
for a department store, has
darker qualities that others
tend to ignore for the sake
of comfort and saving face—
qualities like belief and blood,
heresy and annihilation,
indoctrination and redemption.

As one moves to tip a glass,
one should also remember the
other movement of a sword,
coming down smoothly so as
to sever cleanly the bodies
of the Pagan infidels.

## Red Cross: An Ode to Boxed Wine

The almost-empty polyethylene bladder
of red lies on the kitchen counter, its
nutrients drained slowly from the tap;
having been retrieved from storage, its
life-saving purpose is fulfilled; transfusions
to needy recipients who, upon absorption,
display its therapeutic benefits almost
immediately.

## Re-Orientation

A man sits
inebriated in
a bathroom stall,
forced to scan for
the usual smut,
for the rejects
(of, for, and by)
masculine scum,
for the (unfortunately)
embarrassing
toilet-thoughts and
potty-mouths,
expecting the usual
frustrations (confusions)
of homo-eroticism:

*steve sucks cock*
*alan likes it in the ass*
*for a good bj call bill*

but is surprised by the lack of it.

Finding one mark
in particular quite
shocking

*I ♥ Keith (!)*

he begins to ponder this
coming-out-gesture and
its relation to everything
sexual.

Perhaps, he thinks, the tide has
turned for the better.

But, alas, no
(and not-even-close):

too much booze and
failing to notice the
lack of any urinals
upon entering
was his first mistake.

## Windmills

Their design is deliberate and
foreboding: fleets of alien ships,
packed tightly in attack formation
both upright and sideways
temporarily standing down from
pending orders, strategically arranged,
closing off escape highway-arteries, a
few short breaths away from sealing
our fate with their formidable
weapons of blades and turbines.

## Awareness

A dazed, dry child stands on the sidewalk,
noticing for the first time
the weirdness of the world,
a place where rain falls curiously
only on the other side of the street,
watering the neighbor's lawn
and magnolias,
and getting their
German Shepherd wet.

## Twenty-Five Words (or Fewer)

The four-year old
stood firmly at
the edge of his roof,
wearing his new
Superman costume.
It was going to
be a great Halloween!

*I cannot persuade myself that a beneficent & omnipotent God would have designedly created the* Ichneumonidæ *with the express intention of their feeding within the living bodies of caterpillars, or that a cat should play with mice.*

– from Darwin's letter to Asa Gray (22 May 1860)

## Mr. Snuggles

For some reason (one never
knows why), it was going to
be a good day, and one looked
forward to its promise;

with sun-drenched spirits
and ahead of schedule,
one attempts departure
from home, opening
the door—

only to find
a mouse at one's feet,
also newly departed,
decapitated by the cat
next door.

## **Morpheus**

*for L*

We were informed that the car
flipped and rolled several times,
and that her death was (probably)
quick; it was early morning,
no other cars were around,
and she hadn't been drinking.

When she was small, we would
always end up in the car
late at night to help her sleep.
She was never a good sleeper,
and the ride always worked; she slept
soundly after a nice ride;
it was something we could count on.

Yes, it was just so adorable,
the way she would fall asleep
in our car.

## Doctor

My three-year old looks at me
curiously, sensing that I'm
different now—changed
through diagnosis of a disease
insensitive to bodily boundaries.

*Daddy's sick*, I inform her—
and she grabs her
doctor's kit, which prepares
her for any emergency.

Her mini-stethoscope (along with
my expression) reveals an obvious
fracture in one of my vital organs.

With a doctor's deft hand, she grabs
a plastic syringe, and injects me in
my ear in order to stop the menace
from reaching my diaphragm—
and my death through suffocation.

She concludes her outpatient procedures
by placing her hands on my wrists and
staring deeply into my eyes, commanding
the invader to retreat with her expert
medical concentration.

She asks me, *Feel better, Daddy?*

I answer her the only way I can,
the only way that makes sense,
the only way I know to show my
appreciation for all she will do and
the person she will become—
even though I will never
get to see it:

*A little*, I say.

## My First Time

*for A.L.S.*

They say that you always
remember your first time—
and they're right;
the first time feels different
and you feel different afterward,
and then, you want to do it
every chance you get.

For me, my first time was like
I was born to do it, like
I'd been doing it for a while
and it was all too easy.
Everything fit in the right place
and I knew exactly what to do,
and further, it felt at the time
as if I should be doing it,
and that it almost seemed wrong not to.

And when it was over,
I didn't feel ashamed, or judged,
or exposed; I just thought,
*Oh, so this is how it goes,*
*this is how it's done—*
*and this is what*
*(some) people (have to) do*
*(legitimately).**

*use a handicapped bathroom stall.

## Any Given Sunday

The game was unexpected, but
in some ways inevitable.

A direct and powerful context
provided a playing field, with
unknowing participants already
primed: one terminal patient who
never did believe in God, and one
caregiver who never didn't.

One day the coin was tossed, an
inadvertent comment igniting the
contest, followed by several
conversational moves, thoughts, and
connections—some customary,
some not—occurring over a series
of weeks.

At the game's (and one participant's)
conclusion, it was difficult to determine
the final score—or even to say how
much was at stake.

## Venus Transit

Her journey started long before,
and only recently was she twice
barely detectable: quietly hurtling,
minimally invasive, traveling
millions of miles through light
and darkness for eight years
between exposures, paralleling
a terrestrial journey—new child,
job, city, back-to-back cataclysmic
deaths, and a lethal diagnosis sure
to result in a third not long after
the babe steps out of diapers.

By the time Her voyage is again
noticeable, all those now alive
will have perished—serving as a
reminder that such diagnoses
are not so much lethal as simple
markers for the passage of time.

## Tuskegee

Back in early-1930's Alabama, when
poor rural blacks had no choice in the
matter (and were judged to be expendable),
scientists concealed their diagnoses of
syphilis—a slow and systematic murder of
omission—even after the miracle of
penicillin ten years later may have saved
them. The disease's progression coincided
with an increase in scientific "observations"—
masquerades of inaction thought to be purposeful—
resulting in a "collection of data" from those
who would never benefit from any of it.

Back in late-1930's Minnesota, when the
Yankees (having no choice in the matter) lost
the best first baseman they ever had (who
was clearly not expendable), scientists again
stepped in (not maliciously) with a diagnosis
of another disease both progressive and fatal—
and having no penicillin-equivalent, they greeted
their patient in nicely starched white lab coats,
measured their symptoms as he progressed, and
collected data (knowing their patient would
never benefit from any of it)—

yet another form of
inaction thought to be
purposeful.

## Others

Those who instinctively wonder what
happened to me, offer unsolicited
explanations (for justifying their own
awkward reactions): stroke, tipsiness,
head trauma, car accident, or deafness—
resulting in that annoying sharp increase
in volume—none of which matters
because the confused looks and cringed
eyebrows make me feel exotic and touristy
while speaking in my own living room.

After attending to the actual explanation,
their expression changes. It reminds me
what it's like when I stare into the eye
of a chicken.

## Hook(s)

The disease's wash partly carries
for its carriers a peculiar effect
of hand-muscle atrophy, a curious
digital curvature, mimicking
prehensile-failure-effects more
Pan-like and crocodilic, like those
of James the Jolly commander:
the greatest disbeliever of fairies
this world has ever known.

## Head Games

As I lie very still next to you on our bed,
listening intensely to your thoughts about
the usual life-things, I am focused on
the usual love-things between friend-lovers
of the perfect sort: your intelligence, beauty,
creativity, and the familiar lines that define
your face.

In this timeless-optimal-moment of you,
I can easily forget how
broken I am,
how my perfectly clear thoughts
become nasal
foghorns with occasional comprehensible
syllables when I speak,
how my frail body would collapse
in a heap
if I were to jump
from this bed
and run to the kids
if something happened,
and how you would need to move me
in an emergency,
like a priceless painting
in a house fire.

## Rubber Duckie

A terminal patient, two degrees shy
of complete immobilization, sits and
waits quietly, is cued to raise his arms,
does so mechanically, and thinks how
such crude motion, repetitive and
constrained, reminds him of
assembly-line robots.

There is a system now, a pattern
he follows if he is to avoid smelling
(like urine); he lies down, straining,
and awkwardly raises his knees in
order for her to reach areas usually
reserved for more adventurous
sexual situations.

Upon completion of this lifeless
choreography, he is falsely perceived
afterward to be
unsoiled.

## Helium Day

To those who
end up
being someone
other than
themselves,
reduced,
no longer
recognizable,
forced
into stalled,
aimless, and
unidentifiable
lives which
now personify
dismantled
and dissolved
promises
and parenthetical
limbos—
death indeed
is solace;

this day, all of your
dreams
come true
and
end.

www.ingramcontent.com/pod-product-compliance
Ingram Content Group UK Ltd.
Pitfield, Milton Keynes, MK11 3LW, UK
UKHW041834200726
13854UKWH00003BA/1139

9 781300 172574